What is MASCULINITY? why does it matter? And Other BIG Questions

Jeffrey Boakye & Darren Chetty

For Finley and Otis, and Ellora, with love.

First published in paperback in Great Britain in 2021 by Wayland

Jeffrey Boakye and Darren Chetty have asserted their rights to be identified as the Authors of this Work.

Editor: Nicola Edwards
Design: Rocket Design (East Anglia) Ltd
Artwork by Oli Frape
ISBN 978 1 5263 0815 3
10 9 8 7 6 5 4 3 2 1

Wayland, an imprint of
Hachette Children's Group
Part of Hodder and Stoughton
Carmelite House
50 Victoria Embankment
London EC4Y 0DZ

An Hachette UK Company
www.hachette.co.uk
www.hachettechildrens.co.uk

Printed and bound in China

We would like to thank Shannon Hale for the blog post mentioned on page 33 (https://www.squeetus.com/2015/02/no-boys-allowed-school-visits-as-a-woman-writer.html); Professor Cordelia Fine, Dr Rachel Rosen, Dr Adam Ferner, Dr Rageshri Dhairyawan, Dr Fen Coles.

Picture acknowledgements:
Back cover (left) courtesy of Jeffrey Boakye, (right) Poetcurious; p4 Kathy Hutchins/Shutterstock. com p5 Photo of Andy Williams by Nigel Mackay; photo of Bréanainn Lambkin by Jane Evans; photo of Dave Pickering by Jenny Adamthwaite; photo of Fen Coles by Kerry Mason; photo of Iesha Small by Will Needham; photo of Salena Godden by Olivia Rutherford; p6 Poetcurious; pp8-9 courtesy of Jeffrey Boakye; p10 Getty Images: Warren Little/Staff; p11 Getty Images: Bloomberg/ Contributor; p12 Getty Images: The Print Collector/Getty Images; p14 Jane Evans; p15 Jane Evans; p16 Wikimedia Commons; p20 Jenny Adamthwaite; p23 Shutterstock.com; p24 Will Needham; p26 Wikimedia Commons; p27 (l) Wikimedia Commons; (r) Getty Images: Heritage Images/Contributor; p29 Wikimedia Commons (Gage Skidmore); p32 Kerry Mason; p34 Shutterstock.com /Piotr Zajac; p35 (bl) Wikimedia Commons; (bm) Orion/Kobal/REX/Shutterstock; (br) Shutterstock.com / Krista Kennell; p37 Getty Images: Saul Loeb/AFP/Getty Images; p39 (t) Wikimedia Commons; (b) Wikimedia Commons; p40 Nigel Mackay; p43 Wikimedia Commons; p44 Olivia Rutherford

CONTENTS

WHAT IS MASCULINITY?
WHY DOES IT MATTER?

If you watch the news or read news stories you're likely to come across people discussing masculinity. It's a word that is being used more now than ever before. But what does it mean and why is it in the news so much?

Why a book about masculinity?

People do not all agree on what masculinity is about. Some may be talking about 'toxic masculinity', for example in relation to the behaviour of some powerful men in the Hollywood film industry. Others may be discussing a 'crisis in masculinity', pointing, for example, to the fact that suicide is the biggest killer of men under the age of 50 in the UK. Others still may be arguing that we need to 'reclaim' or 'redefine' masculinity. This can be seen in television programmes such as *Queer Eye*, which encourage men to express their uncertainty about life and their vulnerability.

Many people believe that the stories we are told about how men behave are too narrow, and that they put pressure on boys and men to behave in certain ways. Not only that, they tell boys and girls that men are more important than women and that men should

be in charge – in families, in businesses and in politics for example. So whilst these stories of masculinity are limiting for boys, they are especially damaging for girls and women.

The cast of the Queer Eye *TV series from left to right: Jonathan Van Ness, Karamo Brown, Bobby Berk, Tan France and Antoni Porowski.*

What does 'masculinity' mean?

Our aim in this book is to get you to think about the big questions to do with masculinity. One of those questions is 'what do people mean by masculinity?'. The answer isn't always straightforward. Sometimes people use the word 'masculinity' to describe ways that many men behave and the attitudes they hold. At other times people use the word 'masculinity' to describe the stories we are told about how men *should* behave and act.

If you look up masculinity in a dictionary, you'll find something along the lines of 'masculinity means the qualities considered typical of men'. But there are many more questions we can ask about this, such as:

- Who exactly are these men?

- Does this mean masculinity changes from one man (or one person – can a woman be described as masculine?) to another?

- How common does something need to be to be 'typical'?

- How does something become a typical quality? How can typical qualities change?

- Are the typical qualities of men due to social factors or biology or a combination of both? Should we be dividing actions, attitudes and people into 'masculine' and 'feminine'?

There have always been many ways of being a man. There have often been people who have claimed that there are correct and incorrect ways of being a man. Consequently, whilst some of the people we will discuss in this book are interested in expanding our ideas and representations of masculinity, others are interested in calling into question masculinity and femininity as a way of viewing and organising people.

Talking about masculinity

At times in this book we will write about our own experiences of masculinity, growing up as boys and becoming men. We will also draw on some of the studies of masculinity that have been written by women – indeed, masculinity studies is an area of research that grew out of feminism. We have invited a number of people (see below) to share their perspectives on masculinity in this book and we'll include thoughts on masculinity from other people too. Not everyone agrees on everything but we hope you will find it interesting to see where people agree and disagree.

Iesha Small

Dr Fen Coles

Bréanainn Lambkin

Dave Pickering

Dr Andy Williams

Salena Godden

Darren Chetty

Darren Chetty taught in London primary schools for 20 years and is currently a Teaching Fellow at UCL Institute of Education. He is a contributor to *The Good Immigrant*, edited by Nikesh Shukla. Darren co-writes, with Karen Sands-O'Connor, a regular column on children's literature for *Books for Keeps*. He convenes the *'UK #HipHopEd'* Seminar Series for anyone with an interest in the relationship between education and hip hop culture.

Boys and girls

'Masculinity' was not a word I heard much when I was a child at primary school. However it was often talked about, only using other words.

There were lots of stories about what boys should be like. I learnt that boys should be strong and loud. They should play football and other sports at playtime. If you were not good at sports you might find people suggesting you weren't a 'real boy'.

I remember boys being teased for 'running like a girl' or 'throwing like a girl'. It seemed as though doing anything the other boys said was 'like a girl' was a bad thing. This stopped boys from doing all kinds of things they would have liked to do. And it gave us the mistaken, sexist belief that we were more important than girls.

If I tried something and found I wasn't very good at it, I often gave it up as quickly as possible to avoid ridicule.

But I don't actually think it was just us children making up these silly rules.

> "Looking back ... I didn't try as hard as I could have, just because I was scared other boys would make fun of me. I regret this."

Early definitions

I had a book of old nursery rhymes, including one which said that boys were made of 'Snips and snails and puppy-dogs' tails' (other versions replaced snips with frogs or slugs) and girls were made of 'sugar and spice and all things nice'.

> What are little boys made of?
>   Snips and snails
>   And puppy-dogs' tails
> That's what little boys are made of
>
> What are little girls made of?
>   Sugar and spice
>   And all things nice
> That's what little girls are made of

If boys got into trouble, I sometimes heard adults say 'Boys will be boys'. If girls got into trouble, they would be accused of being 'unladylike'. Adventure stories were almost always about boys, the school football team was only for boys, and even teachers would sometimes tease boys who cried by calling them 'big girls'. I remember sometimes thinking these ideas were odd but they were also very common. It was safest to go along with them, and that's what I did.

Teenage years

At my secondary school, even caring about your schoolwork could mean that other boys might suggest you weren't behaving like a 'real boy' or by this stage 'a real man'. I enjoyed many of the subjects at school, but I also made an effort to appear like I didn't care too much. This took a fair bit of effort. Looking back, it also meant that I didn't try as hard as I could have, just because I was scared other boys would make fun of me. I regret this.

Indeed, admitting to feeling scared – or admitting to feeling almost anything except anger – felt risky in my teenage years. This was the 1980s, the decade of the 'action movie' with star actors who had muscular bodies and who played men of action, not men of words. These were the films most popular with my schoolmates. One common theme was that so-called 'real men' never showed vulnerability – they didn't show they were upset, or confused or unsure about anything.

Taking part

Looking back, the weird thing is that this all didn't just happen to me. I was doing it too. I was quite a good footballer at school and I loved playing in matches. But I could be a show-off about it in ways that makes me embarrassed now. I also loved hip hop. It felt safer to be writing raps than writing poems; safer because nobody would accuse me of not being a 'real man'.

As a teacher I try hard to make sure I'm not passing on the silly rules about how men and women should behave. I'm sure I don't always get it right, but I try and help the children I teach to become happy, caring people who feel free to live their own lives.

Jeffrey Boakye

Jeffrey Boakye grew up in Brixton, south London, with his mother, father and two older sisters. After completing a degree in English literature he worked in editorial and journalism before training to become a teacher. He was married in 2011 and has two sons. In 2017, his first book, *Hold Tight: Black Masculinity, Millennials and the Meaning of Grime*, was published, followed by *Black, Listed* in 2019.

A house of women

Growing up in a household of two older sisters, a very active mother and a father who seemed to be at work all the time, it very much felt like I was raised in a house of women. My mother also worked, a lot, and my sisters are six and seven years older than me, so in my eyes, I lived with adult women making their way in the world in different ways.

My mum had a career in catering that brought in a lot of the household income. My sisters worked part-time jobs before going to university to study complex scientific things that I couldn't spell or pronounce. From an early age I saw that women could have jobs, do further education, hold down careers and be homemakers all at the same time.

Time with my dad

I have fond memories of hanging out with my dad as a young child. I took it for granted, but he really did take the trouble to spend quality time with his only son. Trips to the library, car drives to his friends' houses, weekend visits to his workplace (a textiles factory), buying bikes, buying roller skates. In light of how our relationship would develop in years to come, it's worth stressing that my father was a very active parent in my childhood.

Time with my mother

As my adolescence hit its stride I grew distant from my dad. Family politics crept into our relationship and I became closer to my mother, who was always there for me, keeping me alive, knee-deep in my school life from primary school all the way through to university.

I spent more and more time with my mother. She went to a different church from my father, and I went with her (the photo shows me making my first communion at my mum's church), so that was one huge influence.

Then there was shopping. I would accompany her to the market and supermarket every weekend, long after my sisters got bored of the responsibility, and we became shopping buddies. Along the way, I learned about domesticity, because mum was in charge of running the home, often delegating to my sisters, her deputies.

A patriarchal community

It's fair to say that the culture my parents represented, coming to the UK from Ghana in the 1970s, was very patriarchal. Men like my dad and uncles were given an automatic level of respect within the community. I saw it up close at meal times and at family gatherings. The men would sit in the living room and literally be waited on by the women, who would bring their food on trays and then, when they had finished eating, bring hot soapy water and flannels for them to clean their hands with (most traditional Ghanaian food is eaten by hand).

So on the one hand I saw that women could do anything, earn money, and hold a home together, but on the other I saw men being given higher status than women.

That said, I was lucky enough to be surrounded by fatherly figures who were deeply empathetic and caring, concerned about the futures of the children in the community. 'Uncles', I called them (not always related by blood); men who I felt I could always depend on.

I didn't understand why my dad and uncles should get their food brought to them, and I was usually helping prepare it in the kitchen in the first place. It helped that I was the youngest child, which meant I had little pressure to take up the kind of traditional vocation that firstborn sons are sometimes pressured into: doctor, lawyer, accountant. I was allowed to read books and drift towards English literature. This eventually took me into teaching, which is often considered to be a female profession.

A different dynamic

As a father of two boys myself, I now live in a household with a very different dynamic to the one I grew up in. I feel privileged to have had strong male and female role models in my childhood, something that I feel characterised the community I grew up in.

"I saw that women could do anything, earn money, and hold a home together, but ... I saw men being given higher status than women."

IS MASCULINITY CAUSED BY **TESTOSTERONE?**

One way to explain what people mean by 'masculinity' is to do with the patterns of behaviour seen amongst men and the types of behaviour encouraged and discouraged in men. In other words, what do men do and what are men told they should do? And what, if anything, does testosterone have to do with it?

Physical differences

First of all it's important to point out that men do not all behave in the same way, just as women and intersex people (those whose bodies don't seem to fit the usual definitions of male or female) do not all behave in the same way. However, when we look at large numbers of people, some patterns do emerge.

For example, in athletics, the world record times for men are faster or further than those for women. Of course this does not mean that every man is faster or stronger than every woman – not many men could match the world record time of 2:15:25 Paula Radcliffe set for a woman's marathon in London in 2003. The men's world record for the marathon is a faster time than the women's world record. Some people argue that this is evidence that men's bodies are on average more powerful than women's. But are there other factors to consider?

Paula Radcliffe wins the 2003 women's London Marathon in a world-record time.

Well, yes. Women were not even allowed to take part in the Ancient Olympics. The modern Olympics began in 1896, yet the first women's marathon wasn't until 1984. Clearly, men and women have not been competing on a level playing field.

The role of testosterone

Testosterone is a hormone that is important for reproductive development. It is involved in the development of male sex organs before birth and the changes that happen at puberty, such as voice deepening, increased penis and testes size, and growth of facial and body hair, and, beyond puberty, in muscle growth.

Testosterone is an important hormone to take into account when considering physical differences between men and women. Men's testosterone levels are usually much higher than women's. But is it important for understanding behaviour?

You may sometimes hear people talk about 'testosterone flying about' when describing a group of men being very competitive. People saying this are not making a scientific claim. Also, it's important to recognise that being competitive is not necessarily the same as being aggressive.

For a long time scientists have been interested in the relationship between levels of testosterone and aggressive behaviour, but this is a difficult thing to research and the results haven't been conclusive.

The psychologist Professor Cordelia Fine has looked at the way testosterone is frequently used to explain a wide range of behaviour that is often regarded as 'masculine'. This includes high levels of competitiveness, taking risks, building things and taking charge of situations.

However, Professor Fine concludes, the science just doesn't hold up. She explains that, whilst many behaviours have been called masculine, for some, they are not simply caused by levels of testosterone. The causes are far more complicated. Many of the characteristics that have come to be know as 'masculine' or 'feminine' can be seen in men and women. And where 'masculine' characteristics are more common in men, it is not necessarily due to any biological difference.

As we will discuss later in this book, social reasons for any differences we spot in male and female behaviour are very important. The good news is that, whilst we may well receive messages about what 'real men' do and don't do, we actually have some freedom and responsibility to choose how we behave, rather than it being decided by our hormones.

Traders on the New York Stock Exchange, a highly competitive, male-dominated environment.

ARE THERE
MALE AND FEMALE
BRAINS?

As we're beginning to see, there is an ongoing debate about the exact causes of behaviour and this includes the question of whether there are 'masculine' or 'feminine' ways of thinking.

A false conclusion

There is a long history to the idea that men and women have different brains. In Victorian times, scientists observed that women's brains were, on average, lighter than men's brains. This isn't surprising information as women are, on average, smaller than men. However, scientists at the time made the leap to claiming that this was evidence that men were more intelligent than women. This rested on the idea that the bigger the brain, the more intelligent the person. Scientists have since discovered this is false. But bad ideas in science can still stick around even after they are disproven. Even today you might hear someone being described as having a 'big brain' to mean that they are clever. And you still might hear some people claim that men are more intelligent than women.

London's Charing Cross Hospital in 1901 at the end of the Victorian era. Male surgeons work on a patient in the operating theatre, watched by male medical students.

Similar claims, also disproven, about the superior intelligence of Europeans over Asians and Africans were also being made in the Victorian era. The scientists making these claims were all European men. Women were usually blocked from gaining scientific qualifications – for example, for more than 350 years, men in England had prevented women from qualifying as doctors.

And what's more, at the time these claims were being made, women couldn't vote in the United Kingdom.

Influential ideas

The idea that masculinity is a consequence of a 'male brain' is still around, even without a scientific basis.

In 1992 John Gray's *Men Are From Mars, Women Are From Venus* was published. Gray claimed that men and women were fundamentally different in how they think and communicate. He didn't go so far as to say this was because they had different brains, but many people seemed to interpret his ideas in this way. The book became an international bestseller.

In *Men Are From Mars, Women Are From Venus*, Gray said that men and women differ in all aspects of their lives. He claimed that men and women communicate differently and that they think, feel, react and love differently, too. Gray said that men and women almost seem to come from different planets.

But was Gray right? Well, no. In fact, men are from Earth and women are from Earth.

In 2007, Professor Deborah Cameron, a linguist (someone who studies language),
published *The Myth of Mars and Venus: Do Men and Women Really Speak Different Languages?* She argued that the men and women communicate in similar ways and that where there are differences, this is not because of different brains.

So, there is a long history of men claiming that they have superior brains to women – even though the facts don't support this. These claims have often been made to justify men having important positions of power and control. We'll talk more about this later in the book.

THINK ABOUT

Liz Lochhead's poem 'Men Talk' pokes fun at the idea that men communicate about important things whilst women communicate about unimportant things.

You can read the whole poem in *True Confessions and New Cliches* by Liz Lochhead. If you search for the poem on YouTube, you can listen to a performance of it.

Think about how in the poem Lochhead writes from the perspective of a man who clearly thinks that what men talk about is more important than what women talk about.

How does the poet communicate her anger about the old idea that men are more intelligent and that women should listen and not interrupt or disagree with men?

Bréanainn Lambkin

Bréanainn Lambkin was born in Belfast in 1979. He studied Economics at Glasgow University. In 2000, his son Patrick was born. The family moved to London, where Bréanainn trained to be a Primary Teacher at Goldsmiths, University of London. He loves teaching. He also likes to read and to run, but not at the same time.

Standing out

My parents were different. Born in England, but with a love of Irish culture, they sent my brother, sister and me to the Irish language school in West Belfast, a Catholic, republican area. Despite changing my accent, I stood out a bit. I wore sandals, not Nikes. I had peanut butter sandwiches - brown bread - in the packed lunch. And never a Twix or a bag of Skips. All fine from Mum and Dad's point of view, but a big deal for my classmates and a problem for me. I caught the attention of a few bullies.

Dealing with bullies

I had one close friend at primary school and he also got picked on. My dad told me not to react, not to retaliate – just avoid and ignore. My pal's dad said: here son, this is how to clench your fist. And then it was explained he should pop a jab to the ringleader's nose, not too hard, and the resulting watery eyes would make Bully lose face and back down. The 'not too hard' bit is crucial – neither dad wanted his son to become a violent hard man. At the time, I felt envious: here was my pal's dad showing him how to be tough and manly, while I was getting the 'turn the other cheek' advice. Looking back, I guess both dads were making practical suggestions to minimise violence. We shared the advice we had received and muddled through.

Learning from my dad

I didn't think about it at the time, but my dad was very concerned with political violence back then. He taught history at Belfast's first integrated secondary school, educating Catholics and Protestants together. The movement he was part of believed that segregated schooling was a barrier to future peace. He was never likely to advise fighting fire with fire.

But I still got the message it was OK to be assertive. One football match, chasing

"It was OK to be assertive."

the ball down the wing, the left-back elbowed me hard. I swore loudly, then immediately remembered my dad was on that touchline. Right then, I knew he was going to lecture me about 'foul language' in the car on the way home. Only he didn't. He just gently mocked me for an open goal I'd missed later in the game.

That car journey comes to mind when I hear people give feedback in gendered terms. 'Don't cry like a little girl.' 'Man up and take it on the chin!' You see it on the Internet too: some people seem to take pride in not caring about the feelings of others, only determined to win at 'tough, rational debate'. That day my dad taught me that tone and emotion are important. Our centre midfielder had screamed some humiliating abuse at me when I missed the target (I was still angry about it), but here was my dad encouraging me to see the funny side and saying: keep your cool, concentrate next time.

Learning from my son

For my son, it was secondary school where the bullying started. Late for his voice to break, late for his growth spurt, he got the homophobic ridicule attempting to undermine his masculinity. No serious physical threat that I know of, but lots of changing room verbal abuse in the guise of 'banter'. I offered to call the school, but he said "no". Mostly I just tried to be there to listen if he needed to offload. He fell out of love with football and PE generally. But he did begin joking that he'd like a six-pack.

When he joined a gym to lift weights, I worried it was for the wrong reasons – that social pressure to be buff and strong had gotten to him. Actually it's been a good move. He sticks to a disciplined schedule and he says it calms him. And I think there's a quiet satisfaction there: he may still be slight of build, but he can lift surprisingly impressive weights. He's growing taller and leaving that phase of bullying behind.

And I'm still refining the lessons my dad taught me, especially on communication. If my son's school grades are slipping, and he's feeling stressed and hopeless, my tone of voice is a vital factor in whether he'll respond positively to my advice and offers of help. Our relationship is teaching me how silly it is to instruct someone, 'Be a man'. I cannot control or fix anything for my son. He is becoming a man and he is finding his own way of defining what that is. Sure, his mum and I are part of the conversation, but what manliness means to him is for him to figure out. Like you are you, he's Patrick.

Bréanainn and his son, Patrick

WHAT DO **FEMINISTS** SAY ABOUT **MASCULINITY?**

There's a complicated relationship between thinking of masculinity as what men do and thinking of masculinity as what men are told they should do.

What is patriarchy?

The stories we tell and are told about how men should behave, and the corresponding stories about how women should behave, have received a lot of scrutiny from feminists and students of feminism. Feminists (a term that includes both men and women) reject stories of femininity – that girls and women should, or should not do things simply *because* they are girls and women. They also reject stories of masculinity – that boys and girls should and should not do things simply *because* they are boys and men.

Feminists don't all have the same views on everything, but they tend to agree that

The founding fathers of the USA declared that 'all men are created equal'; they failed to mention women. At the time Black people were enslaved in the U.S. and some of the members of Congress were enslavers.

one way that men have held power over women historically is through a system they call patriarchy – the rule of men. Of course this does not mean that all men are equally powerful. But feminists look at how the laws in many countries gave men more rights and more power than women.

THINK ABOUT

Make a list of some of the heroes in the stories you read and the films you watch. How many of them have the traits associated with 'masculinity'? Qualities like being:

controlling, dominating invulnerable, independent, powerful, competitive, rational and **active**

Women who exhibit these traits however may receive messages that they are being 'unladylike' or 'unfeminine'. Instead, women are rewarded for conforming to stories of 'femininity'. Traits such as being:

nurturing, caring, good at listening, cooperative, emotional, warm and **supportive**

These traits aren't negative – in fact they are very important for becoming a well-rounded person. But feminists argue that associating these traits only with women limits women and men. Under patriarchy, these traits are viewed as important for taking care of children, but not important for being a leader.

Feminists uses the term 'patriarchy' to describe how the most powerful positions in society – such as in politics, law and the media – have been, and continue to be occupied by mostly men and how women have often had less power and fewer rights because of this.

They argue that this has caused the stories of masculinity and femininity – where men are viewed as more important and given more power in the form of rights and money and women have often been limited to taking care of children, men and the home. Most feminists say there have been improvements, usually due to the hard work of women protesting and campaigning for equality. However despite this, they say, patriarchy remains in various forms throughout the world.

Double standards

Feminists argue that men who exhibit the traits listed in the panel (left) have been rewarded by society. Men who do not, have often found themselves mocked or criticised for being 'less masculine' and not being 'real men'. Women who exhibit these traits, however, often receive messages that they are being 'unladylike' or 'unfeminine'. For example, Serena Williams was criticised in 2018 by the chief of the French Open tennis tournament for wearing a bodysuit which she said made her feel 'like a warrior princess' rather than a traditional outfit.

Gender roles defined by patriarchy limit men as well as women, by suggesting they can or should only do some of the things that all people can do. But it is important to recognise that women's traditional gender roles have restricted the amount of power that women have had in politics, in business and in the home.

WHAT IS THE RELATIONSHIP BETWEEN VIOLENCE AND MASCULINITY?

In many ways, the world is a violent place, and in many ways, men control the world. Does this mean that men are violent? Two of the most violent situations the world has ever experienced are the First World War and the Second World War, in which countries flexed their muscles in a lethal game of Who Can Fight The Longest. Both wars were in the first half of the twentieth century.

In control, out of control

During this time, most societies were patriarchal, meaning that they were controlled by men. Since then, countries across the globe continue to spend millions on armies and weapons. Meanwhile, the vast majority of criminals in prison are men, and most violent crimes are carried out by men.

Much of the problem is rooted in the fact that men are encouraged to be in control or powerful or dominant (see page 17). This is the case at almost every level of society: in the home, at work and even between governments, whereby the rules of masculinity state that it is right to be dominant in every situation, all of the time – to win every game, to lead every team. If you are trying to be in control all of the time and you can't (because being in control all of the time is impossible), then what happens?

It's not a problem to be controlling or dominant or in charge some of the time. Many situations need leaders, both male and female. But when the desire to be in control becomes excessive, there comes a temptation to use violence to gain this control. As we shall see in the section 'What is the cost of masculinity?', this violence then becomes a huge problem for everyone, both male and female.

Under pressure

It's important to realise that it's the traditional definition of masculinity that's associated with violence, rather than men themselves. But if there's pressure to conform to a traditional masculine ideal in which violence plays a big part, it might encourage men to behave in a violent, tough way. It's the biggest rule in the age-old 'How to Be a Man' rulebook: be tough, strong and aggressive.

This is so ingrained in the way we think that we even celebrate violence – just look at the entertainment industry, full of movies, video games and music that promote hypermasculinity; tough guys doing tough things. So on to the big question: does the world create violent men?

A history of violence

As a species, it looks like humans are addicted to violence. If you look at world history across different countries and different communities, violence is the common theme, burning angrily throughout the history books. In fact, if you look through world history, you'll find many stories about war, or oppression, or rebellion, or uprising. In a strange sort of way, violence is a language that we all understand, and we speak it well. The communication is simple. If you don't do what I want, I will hurt you. This aggression is a key feature of hard masculinity, the idea that you can use force to get what you want.

It comes down to three things: power, status and hierarchy. When a person, or group of people, demonstrate violence, they are seeking to assert dominance in the sharpest manner possible, creating a situation in which they hold the power.

The idea of being 'masculine' is often linked with being powerful, so much so that men are often expected to be violent in order to be powerful.

Power is power, but there are many ways to gain power through violence. Physical violence is the most obvious, and, maybe because of how young our species is (we've only been around for about 200,000 years) the one we have become most used to. We've also become used to equating masculine power with physical violence, which you can see in all those wars we keep waging on ourselves.

THINK ABOUT

What other kinds of violence are there? Think about environmental violence as one example, where we ravage the planet for natural resources. This attitude is arguably traditionally 'masculine' in the way that it is very aggressive and self-centred. Then there is identity violence where groups assert dominance over other groups based on factors such as race, sexuality and gender.

Dave Pickering

Dave Pickering is a writer, storyteller and podcaster. He's the creator of the solo storytelling show Mansplaining Masculinity, makes the weekly conversation podcast, Getting Better Acquainted, co-produces the magical realist family drama podcast, The Family Tree, and hosts regular true storytelling events. His work has been featured on Resonance FM, Radio 4 and Radio 5 Live, and has been recommended by *The Guardian*, *The Financial Times* and *Time Out*.

I don't remember when I first met my stepdad. But from when I was three years old, he was a part of the family. My early memories of him are positive. He was softly spoken and he gave very solid hugs that made me feel safe. But as I got older, he stopped being a solid and comforting presence and started being someone I feared, someone who wanted me to push down my emotions. I started to feel unsafe in my own skin.

Childhood influences

My stepdad had grown up in a working-class family in Belfast. His father had beaten all the boys with a belt. It was a household where little boys were made of slugs and snails and puppy dogs tails, and girls were made of sugar and spice and all things nice (see page 7). At school he was beaten with a cane. On the streets he had to negotiate the police and the soldiers who would throw you in the cells for nothing. He was always close to explosions and violence. His skin had always been an unsafe skin to live in.

Unwelcome attention

When my mum and my stepdad separated, we moved house. Suddenly I was an English boy in Wales. I had glasses and was acquiring an exciting range of designer acne across my face. I suddenly found myself within the category of swot, geek, nerd.

In an art class in my new school, a boy said I 'looked like a Melvin'. I reacted in a defensive way. The boy and the rest of the class enjoyed this reaction.

Being bullied

The name stuck. I went viral. I would walk down the corridors to jeers of 'Melvin'. Often I'd react, sometimes shouting, sometimes trying to appeal to reason, sometimes crying, sometimes running away. But that isn't sustainable through years of jeers, and as time went on, my reactions became fewer and fewer, and I internalised more and more of it.

As my reactions became less frequent, other techniques were used. New words were added to Melvin: Swot, Geek and Nerd. Bookworm. Foureyes. Minger. Ugly. Disgusting. Pathetic. Fanny. Woman. Sissy. Gaylord. Gay. Homo. Queer. Tramp. And it didn't stop with words. Things were thrown at me. People spat at me. Walking down the corridor, I'd be punched in the back or kicked in the heels.

I didn't think there was anything wrong with being gay or a woman and every time I lost my temper and shouted that I wasn't gay or a woman, I hated myself for acting as if it mattered.

A better future

I don't hate the people who bullied me. I don't hate my stepdad. I mostly manage not to hate myself. But I do hate the systems that surround us. We need to free ourselves and each other from patriarchy, to check our privilege, but also to be free, to feel and express emotions freely and respectfully, to be safe from violence, to support and love each other, feel pretty, express whatever sexuality we have consensually and without shame, seek out, listen to and enjoy stories and perspectives that are different from the ones we have let speak for all of us for so long. The only way to change the situation is to change our approach to the situation. It is built on lies, and it hurts everyone. Let's kill the patriarchy. With love.

THINK ABOUT

How do you think it feels to be bullied?

What do you think Dave means by 'Let's kill the patriarchy. With love'? Can you think of ways to do this? How could this approach help to combat bullying?

"The only way to change the situation is to change our approach to the situation. It is built on lies, and it hurts everyone."

HOW DOES MASCULINITY AFFECT THE WORLD OF **WORK**?

The world of work is often about making money, which can make it a competitive environment. As we've seen, being competitive has traditionally been thought of as a masculine trait. And masculinity is often equated with power, which means that the workplace is a site for power politics. We've come full circle.

The Industrial Revolution

The modern workplace has been created out of social class systems that are linked to industrialisation. In Britain, the Industrial Revolution (roughly from 1760 to 1840) created new groups in the workforce ranging from machine operators to factory managers.

As technology advanced and the scale of manufacture increased, the job landscape saw a huge increase in demand for clerical positions. These included filing documents, processing orders and handling accounts, clerical jobs that were considered higher in status than manual factory work. These were expected to be jobs for men, because it was men who were expected to work while women stayed at home.

Exclusion and inequality

This gender inequality meant that women were largely excluded from the world of professional work, tasked with unpaid domestic work and, more often than not, raising and looking after children. Gender inequality remains a huge problem in the modern workplace, where women have often not been paid as much as men for doing the same jobs.
Some facts:

- In 2018, the Office for National Statistics reported that the gender pay gap for full-time workers was 13.7% in the UK.

- 150 countries have at least one law that treats men and women differently. (World Bank, 2016)

- Globally, an estimated 62 million girls are denied an education. (United Nations)

Masculinity at work

How does masculinity affect the world of work? The workplace has become characterised by traditionally 'masculine' traits relating to being in charge, such as productivity, systemisation, leadership, and progress, all of which can be summarised by the word 'business'.

We even see this in schools, which, unfortunately, have often been like training grounds for male-dominated workplaces, with an obsession with regimented behaviour and 'masculine' appearance in uniform, including shirts, ties and blazers.

Masculinity is so closely linked to the concepts of work and business that we often assume that the work space is mainly a male space. This isn't helped by gender inequality in pay. One problem is the idea of a 'glass ceiling', a limit that women reach in their professional development because of a bias in favour of men. A masculine workplace feels normal because it's been the norm since the Industrial Revolution.

New practices

But times might be changing. Many modern businesses are introducing practices that are distinctively 'softer' than the ways of the traditional, 'masculine' workplace. They have been very successful and include things like:

- Flexible working (instead of strict office hours)
- An emphasis on collaboration and problem solving (instead of sticking to old instructions)
- Empathy (being aware of other people's feelings) and listening (instead of inflexible guidelines)
- Creativity (instead of just setting targets)
- Flat hierarchies, meaning everyone being treated the same (instead of all the power being held at the top)
- Relaxed dress codes (instead of boring suits)

Even though masculinity has been seen as a normal feature of the workplace for a long time, it's looking to be an increasingly poor fit for modern businesses. The world is becoming more connected through digital technology and businesses are having to become more empathetic in order to survive. An example of this is Corporate Social Responsibility, where businesses take greater responsibility for their local community and the environment.

> **"With more women in the workplace and in positions of power and leadership, with the legalisation of gay marriage and the emerging liberation of the LGBTQ community, traditional definitions of masculinity are changing for the better."**
>
> **Andy Dunn, writer**

MY EXPERIENCE

Iesha Small

Iesha Small is Innovation Lead at the education and youth 'think and action-tank' LKMco and an author. Iesha was previously an assistant headteacher and taught maths. She has been a monthly columnist for Schools Week and writes regularly for other major education media outlets. She has also been seconded to the Department of Education and served as a school governor.

Happy times

I have always been a daddy's girl. For part of my early childhood my dad was a long-distance lorry driver; he'd deliver ingredients to Pizza Express restaurants all over England. I remember being so excited during the school holidays when he would sometimes take me with him. I'd climb up high into the cab of his lorry and look down on the cars we passed on the motorway. We'd eat our sandwiches or chicken drumsticks from home out of silver foil at lunch time together in the cab at motorway services and I felt special.

Modelling masculinity

My dad is the first real model of masculinity that I ever experienced, but I wouldn't have thought that when I was a child. I looked up to my dad. From him I learnt dependability and stability. While I was at primary school he was made redundant and took a job that he was massively over-qualified for to make sure that we, his family, could survive. He worked double shifts from early in the morning until late at night and I never heard him complain about it. He knew his responsibilities as a husband and father and did what had to be done.

My dad was a fair, calm and considered presence throughout my childhood. He has never broken a promise to me and, as an adult, I still ask him for measured and objective advice because I value his opinion despite our different perspectives on life.

Facts and feelings

When I became a teenager our relationship shifted. My dad is a product of his generation and upbringing. He is quiet and stoic like his father, my grandad, and like many men of Caribbean heritage. Actions are his thing. I was starting to experience teenage hormones, have more complicated relationships with friends and confusing thoughts about people I (maybe) fancied. Feelings seemed to scare him or make him very awkward so I decided that I'd stick to talking to him about facts and keep certain topics off-limits. Feelings were saved for my nan or my youngest aunty (my mum felt too close to home).

> "My dad can talk about feelings and I hope that I can teach my son that he can too."

Discussions with my son

When I asked my eight-year-old son about how he thought boys were supposed to behave, he said, 'You're just meant to behave the same way as your parents. Like being polite and using manners.' This got me thinking. What are we teaching him about feelings? In my own childhood I had learnt that feelings were private and it was a sign of weakness to express them. My dad never did and neither did other men in my life.

What about children who don't grow up with a dad? My son is the only male in an all-female household but says, 'I feel alright with it.' When I asked him how he could learn about masculinity and how to be a man despite living with two mums and two sisters, he said that he'd learn from the men in our family and friendship group but added 'I don't see the different actions between boys and girls or men and women except the voice.'

Now, I have learnt that it's healthy for me to express feelings to appropriate people. Over time there were other men in my life who it was safe to talk to about feelings, such as my pastor and the boy who became my best friend.

Discussions with my dad

Eventually my dad loosened up a bit too. I recently had a discussion with him that would once have been unthinkable. What started off as a quick birthday call ended up as a wide ranging discussion about trust, intimacy and our own quirks and mistakes in relationships with our partners. This was all interspersed with the general laughter and mickey-taking that is a constant feature of our relationship. My dad can talk about feelings and I hope that I can teach my son that he can too.

THINK ABOUT

What have you learnt from the people that you live with about masculinity and what it means to be a man or a boy? How have they shown you? Do you agree with them?

WHERE HAVE IDEAS
ABOUT MASCULINITY
COME FROM?

We've said that the popular ideas about masculinity – about how men should behave – have come from the stories and messages we hear. But where do these stories and messages come from? The answer to this question is not straightforward, but one important (perhaps the most important) place that stories about masculinity come from is the world of politics.

Let's look at a few examples.

France in the 1800s

Napoleon Bonaparte (right) was a French military leader and emperor who conquered much of Europe in the early nineteenth century. His Napoleonic Code (or The Civil Code of 1804), gave an overview of the laws and influenced many countries in Europe and beyond. The code stated that a husband owed protection to his wife and a wife owed obedience to her husband. It also gave men but not women civil and political rights. A woman was not allowed to buy property without the written permission of her husband or father.

1920s Italy

In Italy in the 1920s, Benito Mussolini, leader of the National Fascist Party, came to power. He had soon abandoned democracy in the country and transformed Italy into a fascist state.

Mussolini (centre) with Hitler (left)

In order to establish Italy as a strong nation, Mussolini promoted traditional gender roles, which he linked back to ancient Rome. He claimed there were proper mental and physical qualities for being a real man and claimed that the rightful role of men was to be warriors, saying 'war is to man what maternity is to the woman'. A woman's role, according to Mussolini, was to stay at home and raise children and a man's was to work and to fight for the nation. Mussolini also made homosexuality illegal. During the Second World War, Mussolini's Italy fought with Hitler's Nazi Germany. Mussolini promoted himself as the strong father, the patriarch, of the nation.

"Never before and never afterward has masculinity been elevated to such heights as during fascism."

George Mosse, historian

Whilst fascism produced some of the most extreme messages about masculinity, it was not the only political movement to have strong views on how men should act and behave.

Soviet era communism

The Communist Party of the Soviet Union put forward the idea of the New Soviet Man. Featuring in propaganda posters of the period, such as the one below, ideal masculine qualities included being healthy, muscular, knowledgeable and hardworking, as well as being selflessly dedicated to the Soviet Union.

Latin America in the 1960s

In the 1960s, feminists in Latin America began to write about machismo. This word described the expectation that boys and men should be macho, which was explained as being strong, courageous, wise leaders. However, it also revealed the opinion that men were superior to women, and that to be male meant being aggressive and even violent.

WHAT EFFECT DO IDEAS
ABOUT MASCULINITY
HAVE ON RELATIONSHIPS?

Making connections

There are many different types of relationship. We may have parents, carers, other relatives, friends and acquaintances (people we know, but not very well). There are also relationships with people that we don't necessarily choose to spend time with, such as teachers, classmates and work colleagues. Some of these relationships may last a lifetime and some may be much shorter. As we grow older we may develop romantic or intimate relationships and in time these may become sexual relationships.

A harmful effect

Some of the traditional ideas about masculinity can impact the relationships boys and men have.

If boys grow up believing that they shouldn't express when they are upset or unhappy – if they are told, and tell each other to 'man up', to 'grow a pair', to 'be a man' or to 'stop being a girl', then this might make them less likely to talk to friends and family when they are finding life difficult. If this happens they are less likely to get the help and support they need at difficult times. 'Putting on a brave face' is unlikely to be the best way to get through times when you are feeling that things are difficult. We are under no obligation to tell people all of our innermost feelings and we may have very good reasons for keeping some things private, or sharing only with those closest to us. But it can be helpful to know that 'suffering in silence' isn't necessary, and that it can do more harm than good.

In 2016, 75 per cent of all UK suicides were male. Whilst the precise reasons for this are no doubt complicated, many people think the idea that 'real men' are 'the strong, silent type' contributes to this. The Campaign Against Living Miserably (CALM) is an award-winning charity dedicated to preventing male suicide. Its patron, the rapper Professor Green, has said: "Asking for help when things go bad is what everyone should be able to do, whatever their gender."

Selfish behaviour

Another issue we have discussed in this book is how stories about so-called real men are often about men taking control of situations, getting their way and thinking about themselves only and not about the people around them. If people act in this way they are less likely to listen to how others are feeling. At the most extreme,

they might even not think of others as people just like them, but rather as things that they can use.

If you think that's how a friend thinks about you – if they won't ever listen to you, if they're not interested in sharing and if they try to make you do things you don't want to do – then they are probably not a friend in the real sense of the word.

If those things are to do with your personal space and with your body, then they are likely to be doing something that is harmful, perhaps even illegal. In law, consent is agreeing to do something and having the capacity to agree to do something. The age of consent for sexual activity in the UK is 16.

"We have seen powerful men in Hollywood and elsewhere, finally held accountable for sexual harassment and assault. This encouraged me to come forward with my own experiences and reflect on the cult of toxic masculinity that exists in our society. As a man, I was taught my entire life, that I must control the world."

Terry Crews, actor and former American football player addressing the US Congress in 2018

Everyone has the right to feel safe and to live their life free from all forms of abuse. If you have been affected by any of the issues covered in this book, there are people and places you can go to for help. There is a list of helplines and organisations on page 47.

HOW DOES **STEREOTYPING** AFFECT CHILDREN?

If 'masculine' behaviour is something that can be taught, then childhood is the place where the rules of masculinity are introduced, practised and learned.

Gender stereotypes

There are obvious biological and physical differences between boys and girls, but gender is far less obvious. Gender is something that is constructed and it can be performed, like a role in a play. For children, gender roles – the way men and women are expected to act – are learned early. A lot of it starts with socialisation, beginning with how children are treated by the adults in their lives. Take the colours of baby clothes, for example. The idea that pink is 'a girl's colour' and blue is 'a boy's colour'. This is a stereotype with no basis in fact.

Clothing is just one example. Beyond this, the way that adults treat boys and girls in different ways also affects how we are taught gender roles. Society plays a huge role in creating gender stereotypes.

For boys, it's the pressure to be 'masculine': superheroes, sport and physical aggression.

For girls, it's the pressure to be 'feminine': princesses, passivity and being beautiful.

We also see gender stereotyping in products for children, where toys targeted separately at boys and girls (with pink and blue packaging to match) are a common feature of shopping aisles and supermarket shelves.

Mixed messages

For men of the future, toys have become an area in which 'masculinity' is encouraged. Popular boys' toys include an unsurprising selection of macho items: cars, trucks, trains, construction sets, gadgets and gizmos, as well as the more violent weapons and action figures. Meanwhile, girls are offered dolls and fashion-focused accessories. Clothes also reflect gender stereotypes, featuring messages about being strong, clever or active for boys and about looking sparkly or pretty for girls.

> **"Research by the Institution for Engineering and Technology in 2016 found toys with a science, technology, engineering and maths element were three times as likely to be targeted at boys. Only nine per cent of engineers in the UK are women."**
>
> **A newspaper report in the *London Evening Standard***

Starting early

Much of this gender stereotyping begins in childhood, when key choices over what boys and girls 'should' and 'shouldn't' do are prompted by society at large. For example, boys are more often encouraged to get involved in physical activities and sports than girls are. The competitive nature of sport has led many to think it is more of a male thing to do. This stereotyping is reflected in the world of professional sport, in which the male versions of some popular sports are invested in far more than the female equivalent. (Just think how much more coverage the FIFA World Cup for men's football gets compared to the FIFA Women's World Cup).

If children see mainly men taking part in sport at a professional level, then they might start thinking that sport is for boys. Cordelia Fine (see page 11) talks about the idea of children being 'gender detectives'. This means that when we are children, we work out what gender is by looking for clues as to how adults create a world for boys and girls. We get very good at this very early.

These trends have led to a kickback against child-centred stereotyping. For example, the Let Toys Be Toys campaign seeks to encourage manufacturers and retailers to stop gendering children's toys in a bid to promote gender equality.

Limits on lives

Many people believe that boys would benefit from being separated from masculine conditioning. It makes sense when you think about the social problems linked to masculinity that affect boys and men in particular, including mental health problems and an increased risk of suicide in later life. To limit boys' experiences of play to a narrow range of 'masculine' experiences increases the pressure to conform to these stereotypes in later life. This is where gender can be uncomfortable and restrictive. If boys don't think they can be caregivers or creatives, while girls don't think they can be problem-solvers or manual workers, the future of the world and work starts to look bleak.

THINK ABOUT

Have you ever been treated in a particular way because of your gender?

What kind of toys were you given when you were younger?

Have you ever seen adults treating boys and girls differently?

Dr Fen Coles

Dr Fen Coles is co-director of Letterbox Library, a not-for-profit children's booksellers which specialises in inclusive and diverse books. She used to work in the women's and LGBTQ rights sector and she has a PhD in Interdisciplinary Women's Studies.

Rules and restrictions

Growing up, I never felt I had much to benefit from ideas about 'femininity' and 'masculinity'. Everything I heard about 'femininity' was either pretty negative – basically instructions on how to take a back seat – or sounded like a performance – how to glam up. 'Masculinity' was something my brothers did. The rules were equally restrictive but they at least seemed to describe positive qualities: being brave, ambitious and strong.

It was very clear that 'femininity' was for girls and 'masculinity' belonged to boys. And to 'do' these properly you also had to be straight. This message was driven home to me when, after coming out, some of the homophobic language I heard sent this message: lesbian = not 'feminine' = not a 'real' woman. Words like 'geezer bird', 'butch', 'bull dyke' all suggested I had become … like a man? Meantime, my queer male friends were assaulted with words like 'sissies',

'pansies', 'nancies'. Because 'femininity' and 'masculinity' don't just tell you how to be a 'real' woman or man; they also set out rules about your sexuality. Sexism and homophobia go hand in hand.

When I joined Letterbox Library back in 2005, I wondered whether I had stepped into some sort of 1950s vortex; the book industry seemed to be full of really outdated ideas about gender. Lots of toy shops at that time were dividing their aisles with boys/girls and blue/pink signage. And something very similar was going on with children's books, with some publishers going so far as to actually say, 'For Boys' or 'For Girls' on the book covers. That's when I started to understand that what I'd thought were 'qualities' associated with 'masculinity' (see list above!) were actually limiting boys.

Wrecking reading

You thought reading a book was an innocent gesture? Free from the gender police? Not so. Here are just some of the received ideas about 'masculinity' which totally wreck the book world for boys: boys don't read; black boys and working-class boys definitely don't read; boys won't read books with female protagonists; boys only read books about sports/gangs/war/more sports; boys only read books about boys; boys who do read are 'sensitive' a.k.a. 'girlie' or gay (with the suggestion that both are very bad things to be).

As a bookseller, I can promise you that all of the statements above are myths. But they risk being self-perpetuating myths. And they can be pretty damaging too. For example, in a 2015 blog (see page 2), children's author, Shannon Hale, posted: "The belief that boys won't like books with female protagonists ... the shaming that happens when they do ... the idea ... that boys aren't expected to understand ... the female population of the world ... this belief directly leads to ... a culture that tells boys and men, it doesn't matter how the girl feels, what she wants. She is here to do what you want. No one expects you to have to empathise with girls and women." Wow.

Redefining definitions

Right now there is a new wave of books coming out which are challenging ideas about 'masculinity' and about what it means to be a boy/man. I hope this will take us to a new place where those traditional ideas will be pretty meaningless or at least won't limit our lives. Maybe being 'masculine' will just come to describe someone wielding an axe (in an appropriate place) and being 'feminine' will describe someone wearing sequins (also in an appropriate place) but the key thing is that anyone - male, female, genderfluid, trans - can wield that axe or put on sequins or do both at the same time. But then if that was the case, the words 'masculine' and 'feminine' wouldn't really mean anything anyway ... So, maybe we could just ditch them?!

"I hope this will take us to a new place where those traditional ideas will be pretty meaningless or at least won't limit our lives."

THINK ABOUT

Have you ever felt as if there are some books you should or shouldn't read because you are a boy or a girl?

Do you think we need terms like gender/masculinity/femininity or can we do away with them?

HOW HAS **MASCULINITY** AFFECTED THE WAY WE SEE OURSELVES?

If you were an alien visiting planet Earth and you wanted to know what it means to 'be a man', how to be 'masculine' and what 'masculinity' looks like, popular culture would be a good place to start.

Coded in conflict

Masculinity can be seen in lots of cultural products, from movies to music, sport to literature, art to computer gaming and everything in between. Often, ideas of what masculinity is, are based in conflict and aggression. As we have already seen when we looked at masculinity and violence (pages 18-19), the First and Second World Wars were huge moments of sustained military action that took millions of men from countries all over the world and turned them into soldiers. This helped create masculinity codes of aggression, bravery and violence that characterised the masculine ideal deep into the twentieth century and beyond.

Cinematic stereotyping

Cinema has always been a reflection of idealised masculinity, offering up a long line of male heroes who conform to masculine stereotypes. After the Second World War there emerged the figure of the war hero, a man who fights bravely in battle and seeks to save the day. Meanwhile, the spy became another popular masculine archetype. The fictional British Secret Service agent James Bond (shown here as played by Daniel Craig) was resourceful, suave,

sophisticated, tough, and, importantly, irresistible to women. James Bond has become a huge cinema franchise, with dozens of films to date, based on novels by Ian Fleming written in the 1950s. With James Bond films continuing to be made, it's clear that the masculine codes of old are going nowhere any time soon.

Supernatural heroes

Meanwhile, a more colourful kind of hypermasculinity was being sketched on the pages of comics in the 1950s and 1960s, when the 'superhero' emerged. As the name suggests, the superhero (originally male) was a hero of supernatural proportions. Early examples such as Superman were adorned with physical abilities of strength, speed and agility beyond the ordinary person, a trend that would become a template for all superheroes to come. Elsewhere, Batman gave us a masked crusader fighting for justice, while Marvel Comics opened the lid on a whole cast of superpeople who embodied masculine ideals of strength. Superheroes have become a major feature of the Hollywood movie machine, with big-budget reimaginings of twentieth-century comics drawing audiences to the cinema in their millions.

Muscles and movies

As we moved into the 1980s, we saw a new type of superhero. He had massive muscles, often carried huge guns, and could be very violent in his quest to save the world. Suddenly, men who looked like they had been drawn with extra muscles on began to dominate cinema screens in so-called 'action movies', none more so than the Austrian bodybuilder Arnold Schwarzenegger (see below). His success as a super-masculine action star eventually took him all the way into US politics when he was elected the governor of California between 2003 and 2011. A bodybuilder is someone who works hard to make their muscles as big as possible. A governor is a political leader. It says a lot about how much we like masculinity that one could become the other.

The one thing that seems to link these expressions of masculinity in popular culture is aggression; a theme that keeps recurring in the masculinity debate.

At the same time, however, the 1980s saw a softening of hard masculinity in the worlds of music and popular entertainment, which we'll explore further on page 39.

Arnold Schwarzenegger, from bodybuilder to movie star and politician

WHAT IS THE COST OF MASCULINITY?

Masculinity applies a constant pressure on boys and men to be the best. The rules of the masculinity game state that the most successful men are the ones with the most status. They're the most powerful, the strongest, the most influential, generally the most alpha. In fact, wanting to be the 'alpha male' – the male at the top of the hierarchy tree – is a phrase that is often used in conversations about men in relation to other men.

The cost for men

This pressure to be the best affects every aspect of life. Have the biggest muscles, drive the fastest car, make the most money, wear the nicest clothes, tell the funniest joke, be the best player, get the best exam results, have the best job … the list goes on. Men are under pressure to be impressive in pretty much every avenue of their existence, and it's an impossible expectation to live up to.

The result of this pressure is a deep insecurity over living up to expectations that cannot be met, turning into anxiety. This is where the true cost of the masculinity ideal starts to show. For men, who often can't escape masculine expectations, failure to be alpha is failure full stop, and the resulting damage to their mental health can be catastrophic.

The evidence is staggering. As we've seen, figures from the Office for National Statistics showed that in 2016, suicide was the most common form of death for men aged between 20 and 49 in England and Wales. The same report said that 75 per cent of all recorded suicides in the UK were male.

Internationally, the figures are similar, with men consistently outstripping women in suicide frequency. Does this mean that there is a global crisis in male mental health? What is it that is driving so many men to take their own lives at a higher rate than women?

Clearly, too many men, and boys, are looking at themselves in a world that says 'man up', falling short of the impossible ideal, and spiralling into the worst excesses of depression and anxiety.

And masculinity isn't just leading men to harm themselves. Research shows that while the number of female prisoners in England and Wales has dropped since 1901, the number of male prisoners has risen dramatically. To put it simply, men are committing more crimes. This is likely to be because of social reasons rather than biological differences (see page 11).

The cost for women

We've already seen how masculinity negatively affects women in the world of work. It also has a far-reaching negative impact on women in other ways. Domestic violence is a problem that has existed throughout history across countries, in which women in the home are victim to excessive male control that becomes violent. This violence can take the form of physical or emotional abuse, leaving victims at the mercy of men seeking to be dominant. A recent crime survey found that in the UK:

26 per cent of women aged 16 to 59 have experienced some form of domestic abuse since the age of 16

7.5 per cent of women (1.2 million) experienced domestic abuse in the year up to March 2017, compared to 4.3 per cent of men (713,000)

(Office for National Statistics)

The cost for the planet

On a global scale, masculinity might be responsible for the biggest, most dangerous threat to life we can ever imagine: war. The pressure for countries to be strong and show power over other nations can easily lead to international conflict. Add weapons of mass destruction to the mix and the picture becomes even more terrifying. Many countries spend time and resources on nuclear arms development, a process which is linked to masculine ideals of strength. It's a terrifying thought, but the next world war could be the result of macho refusal to back down in an argument.

The pressure to be tough is a dangerous game for individuals and communities alike, if not the entire planet.

In January 2018, President Trump posted this tweet, boasting about the USA's nuclear weapons in response to North Korean leader Kim Jong-un's claims about his country's own nuclear capabilities:

> **"I too have a Nuclear Button, but it is a much bigger & more powerful one than his, and my Button works!"**
>
> **-@realDonaldTrump**

Kim Jong-un and Donald Trump (shaking hands, centre) meet in 2018.

WHAT DOES SEXUALITY HAVE TO DO WITH MASCULINITY?

When it comes to masculinity politics, sexuality is a major concern. Men are often encouraged to have sex with women, which is considered a very normal thing for men to do. One of the biggest rules of modern masculinity is that a 'real' man is heterosexual, and physically attracted to women. Homosexuality challenges this idea on a basic level because it says that men can be sexually attracted to other men.

Nothing new

For as long as there have been people, there have been men who are sexually attracted to men and women who are sexually attracted to women. Unfortunately, homosexuality has been a target of prejudice across history. In many countries it has been, or still is, illegal to be homosexual, with gay people facing prejudice and discrimination. The role of 'toxic masculinity' in this is clear, as it promotes the idea that 'proper' masculinity cannot include men who aren't attracted to women.

Public and private

Nowadays, it's not unusual to see gay men in the public eye, but, in many stereotypically masculine environments, homosexuality remains something of a social taboo. In professional sports such as football for example, gay men are rarely seen, despite the fact that they must surely exist. Meanwhile, the phrase 'coming out of the closet' is still used to describe gay men choosing to make their sexuality public, suggesting that homosexuality is still often hidden until gay men are confident enough to reveal their true feelings to the world.

Is masculinity responsible for this? Pressures to conform to expectations about what a 'proper man' should be can make it difficult for gay men to 'come out', especially if they are in a community in which gay men are a minority and if they feel they are under threat from homophobic attitudes and behaviour.

Gareth Thomas (below), the former captain of the Wales national rugby team, came out as gay in 2009 and now campaigns for LGBTQ rights. In 2018 he spoke out after becoming the victim of a homophobic attack in Cardiff. In a video posted to his Twitter page he said: "There's a lot of people out there who want to hurt us. But unfortunately for them, there's a lot more who want to help us heal."

New men

Liberalism is a point of view that is open to difference and welcoming of different types of people. Increasingly, liberal ideals mean that homosexuality is becoming less of a social taboo in many parts of the world, as mainstream society accepts that men can still be men if they are gay. In the 1980s, the concept of the 'New Man' emerged, describing a new kind of man with a softer masculinity, more in tune with his emotions than the traditional man of previous decades. The 'New Man' was a challenge to masculinity norms, suggesting that a man could still be a man even if he was 'caring, sensitive and non-aggressive' (as the Oxford English Dictionary put it).

One interesting development in modern masculinity is a growing concern with body image, particularly among young men and adolescents. Research in 2012 from the Centre for Appearance Research at the University of the West of England found that over 80 per cent of men are anxious about their body image. This includes concern about muscles, weight and hair loss.

These pressures can be linked to the '90s concept of the 'metrosexual' man. The word metrosexual is a combination of 'metropolitan' and 'sexual'. It refers to a man who cares a lot about his appearance and personal grooming in ways that have previously been usually associated, stereotypically, with women.

"I think masculinity is bravado against the mystery of the universe of women. It's just a fear of not knowing what women have that's so powerful. It's this shield they put up to try to get closer."

K.D. Lang

Dr Andy Williams

Dr Andy Williams is a Consultant Physician in Sexual Health and HIV Medicine at The Royal London Hospital. His work focuses on male sexual health, care of people living with HIV and medical education.

A confusing reaction

I was six years old. I know that because I can vividly remember the classroom where it took place. The teaching assistant was standing in front of me pointing, laughing and beckoning for others to join her in the hilarity of the Cabbage Patch Doll I had chosen to present for 'Bring Your Favourite Toy Day'. I wasn't laughing, I wasn't upset, I was confused. It made no sense to me that this was funny. She told me that this was a girl's toy and I shouldn't be playing with it.

Feeling different

There were other similar episodes over the course of my primary school days. These and my interest in school plays, choosing to chat with the girls at playtime and being outstandingly bad at every sport we were required to take part in all meant that I realised I was different from the other boys. I am incredibly fortunate that for the most part of my childhood being different wasn't a bad thing. I wasn't treated negatively nor as a point of amusement. I was just me, a boy in the class with everyone else.

Towards the end of my teenage years I realised that I was gay which brought a huge sense of shame and embarrassment. I was at medical school and I didn't know anyone who was gay, certainly not any doctors. Could you even be a doctor if you were a gay man? I felt very strongly that I needed to keep this information as secret as possible and have a tight hold on who knew it.

Months and years of secrecy and sometimes unhappiness followed but very slowly things changed. I told my friends and I told my family – my dad said "you probably feel like you've invented the wheel, but you haven't". How right he was; of course men who are different are everywhere, but at that time their difference was never spoken about, never championed.

Work and family life

I'm now a Consultant working in Sexual Health and HIV Medicine in London. I'm also a dad; my partner and I adopted our son in 2015. My work is mainly focused on male sexual health and wellbeing, allowing all men to understand their bodies and be able to make safe and consensual choices. There is still a lot of work to be done to improve relationship and sex education in schools and to ensure that people from all cultures, religions and backgrounds are able to make informed choices in their relationships and have an understanding of their physical and emotional development.

In my work and social networks I mix with men of all ages, men with differing physical abilities and men who have experienced mental ill health, straight men, gay men, trans men, men born in the UK and men who have migrated from other parts of the world, men who have children, men who have chosen not to have children, men who would dearly love to be fathers but are not, men who wouldn't miss a football match and men who wouldn't miss a Beyoncé concert. Of course all men are different, but some men's differences are unfortunately still more widely accepted than others.

I would like to think that the world is changing and that expectations of boys and men to pursue traditional male roles and interests are shifting. My hope is that when my son and nephews reach adulthood, society will be free from assumptions, allowing men to live their lives authentically, supported and encouraged by those around them.

"I would like to think that the world is changing and that expectations of boys and men to pursue traditional male roles and interests are shifting."

THINK ABOUT

How have you reacted to people whose families, hobbies or abilities are different from yours? How might that have made them feel?

WHAT IS THE FUTURE
OF MASCULINITY?

Will it prove to be increasingly incompatible with the modern world?

Some facts:

- In marriage, tradition dictates that women take their husband's last name, a tradition that for some, continues until the present day.

- Within families in many cultures, money is traditionally only left to the eldest son. If there are no sons, it might be passed on to another male family member.

- In many parts of the world women have been denied the right to vote in political elections. In some countries, it is still very difficult for women to vote because they might need permission to leave the home, or there might be strict rules set out by men in the community.

- Women are often paid less than men for doing the same jobs, in lots of different types of work. The 'gender pay gap' is a name given to the difference in average pay between men and women.

- Men are still sometimes seen as 'the head of the family' or 'breadwinner', meaning that they are expected to provide for the family.

So what is the future of masculinity? Will it become more flexible? Will it become less demanding of men and boys than in the past? Can masculinity exist in a world in which toxic, macho attitudes are being challenged and men are becoming more and more accountable for their behaviour?

Speaking out

Challenging the values associated with traditional masculinity is nothing new, but we might be getting better at it. For example, the '#MeToo' movement has put toxic masculinity under a very public spotlight, exposing men who have exploited women. As more and more women speak about their experiences of sexism, the problems of toxic masculinity in a male-dominated world are revealed.

Gender inequality

But historically, masculinity has always stuck fast, with men remaining unfairly advantaged, and things are still lopsided in the favour of men. The vast majority of governments, businesses and corporations, the legal system, the media, sport and entertainment, are all led by men. Gender inequality remains a huge problem, with women paid less on average than their male counterparts and massively underrepresented in the upper levels of the professional world.

At the same time, women and girls in many parts of the world lack basic human rights, denied the opportunities offered to boys and men. This includes education, which is the single most important factor in self-empowerment. Figures from UNESCO show that while global literacy rates have increased overall since the mid 1980s, there has been a constant gap between male and female rates of literacy. The gap is closing, but there's still work to be done. The tradition of men dominating the world is preventing women from being treated fairly.

Big questions

Does this mean that modern masculinity promotes gender inequality? Will masculinity have to crumble if true equality is ever going to be reached? Are men of the future destined to a life of emotional frustration because of the pressure to be 'manly'? And will they eventually reject these pressures as a result?

These are big questions with no easy answers. We know that masculinity can be damaging in different ways. For boys, masculinity creates pressure to be tough and emotionless, which can ultimately lead to loneliness, isolation and mental health problems. For men, masculinity is a weight that must be carried at all times. For women, masculinity impacts how men treat them, and justifies stories of femininity which restrict them. And for society at large, masculinity gets in the way of gender equality and gay rights, whilst also encouraging violence and toxic attitudes.

Redefining masculinity

Maybe the future of masculinity is all about what kind of world we want for ourselves. If we are happy with aggression and control and emotional inflexibility then traditional masculinity is probably the way forward. If there's a need for change, and many people would agree that there is, then it just might be time for a change, starting with our ideas of what masculinity should be.

It's a good thing that masculinity is finally being redefined. In 2011, the mental health charity MIND and the Men's Health Forum (MHF) launched the first ever set of guidelines looking at the mental health needs of men and boys, aiming to improve mental health care and services for men and boys in England. People are offering new ideas about what it means to be a man and widening masculinity to include a healthier range of attitudes. This might mean that we are escaping traditional gender roles that many people struggle to fit into.

"If one man can destroy everything, why can't one girl change it?"

Malala Yousafzai, human rights activist and advocate of girls' rights to education

Salena Godden

Salena Godden is one of Britain's foremost poets whose electrifying live performances and BBC radio broadcasts have earned her a devoted following. She is the author of *Under The Pier, Fishing in the Aftermath: Poems 1994-2014*, the literary childhood memoir *Springfield Road* and *Shade* published in the award-winning anthology *The Good Immigrant*. Here is an extract from a piece Salena wrote which explores different definitions of masculinity.

Masculinity is free to run and play in the dirt. Masculinity won't wear pink. Masculinity isn't stuffed into an uncomfortable dress and told to sit up straight. Masculinity spreads its legs and slouches. Masculinity is seen and heard. Masculinity is encouraged to ride bikes and climb trees. Masculinity pulls the wings off butterflies. Masculinity says boys will be boys. Masculinity rips its trousers. Masculinity bloodies its nose. Masculinity will not cry in public. Masculinity does not want to talk about the events leading up to the ripped trousers and the bloody nose. Masculinity keeps its mouth shut because Masculinity knows what's good for it.

Masculinity has grown a beard.

Masculinity is the leader. Masculinity leads the gang. Masculinity is a soldier. Masculinity hunts and Masculinity kills animals for sport. Masculinity has a right to bear arms. Masculinity works out in a gym to build muscles that are masculine. Masculinity looks after itself. Masculinity is not weak. Masculinity is big and strong and brave. Masculinity is not a mummy's boy. Masculinity is not a cry baby. Masculinity will not cry in public.

Masculinity can be a gentleman.

Masculinity is your father and your brother. Masculinity is the boss. Masculinity is the lord and master. Masculinity is the captain of the ship. Masculinity is in control. Masculinity is at war. Masculinity is in conflict.

Masculinity won't take no for an answer.

Masculinity won't let you finish your sentence. Masculinity explains your own words back at you. Masculinity sends you to the kitchen to make a cup of tea like a good girl. Masculinity is red-blooded.

Masculinity eats double portions because Masculinity has an appetite. Masculinity is expected to have a huge appetite.

Masculinity is the headline act.

Masculinity is the lead storyline. Masculinity is the lead role. Masculinity is prime time television. Masculinity is promoted. Masculinity is the winner. Masculinity is in adverts that advertise these confusing and contradictory versions of Masculinity. Masculinity is on the front page of the newspapers. Masculinity is corrupted.

Masculinity gets lost in translation.

Masculinity is paid well. Masculinity is paid twice as much. Masculinity gets praise for being Masculinity. Masculinity is confident. Masculinity is James Bond. Masculinity is for real men. Masculinity is a cowboy. Masculinity is the superhero. Masculinity smokes a fat cigar. Masculinity plays golf. Masculinity has a yacht. Masculinity has a fast car. Masculinity has money and power. Masculinity has a hairy chest. Masculinity is gonna make you a star.

Masculinity is a silverback gorilla.

Masculinity is hungry. Masculinity slouches at the table and eats in silence. Masculinity doesn't talk. Masculinity won't listen. Masculinity leaves its socks on the floor for someone else to pick up. Masculinity is catered for. Masculinity is pandered to. Masculinity has choice. Masculinity is amplified. Masculinity is dominant. Masculinity says it has always been this way, so why change now?

Masculinity is confusing.

Masculinity says it wouldn't like it if Masculinity treated its sister or daughter like this. Masculinity is uncomfortable with public breastfeeding. Masculinity won't talk about periods. Masculinity isn't going to talk to a therapist. Masculinity won't go and see a doctor. Masculinity has too much Masculinity to use a moisturiser or even sun block. Masculinity has too much Masculinity to ask for help. Masculinity is misunderstood.

Masculinity is fragile.

Masculinity is Hollywood. Masculinity is the centre of the books you read and the music you buy. Masculinity is the law. Masculinity is religion.

Masculinity is flawed.

Masculinity is more than a word. Masculinity can be what you want it to be. Masculinity is not alone and was never alone. Masculinity is part of a beautiful spectrum. Masculinity shows fear. Masculinity tells the truth. Masculinity opens its arms. Masculinity wants equality. Masculinity stops being a cliche of Masculinity. Masculinity is sharing. Masculinity wears a dress. Masculinity wears lipstick. Masculinity can nurture and protect. Masculinity is a teacher. Masculinity respects women. Masculinity is kind and considerate. Masculinity can weep and fail and ask for help. Masculinity breaks. Masculinity is broken. Masculinity is learning and growing and changing. Masculinity is multi-dimensional and multi-coloured. Masculinity is mortal.

Masculinity is human.

GLOSSARY

archetype – a common example of a certain type of person

body image – what a person thinks about their own body, usually influenced by standards that are set by society

conditioning – being influenced into behaving or acting in a certain way

consensual – describes something that is done with the agreement of everyone involved

democracy – a system of government in which power is held by elected representatives of the population

domesticity – life at home taking care of yourself and others who live with you

empathetic – having the ability to understand the feelings of other people

fascist – describes a system of power in which a state is led by a dictator and any opposition is put down, often violently

feminism – the belief that women and men should have equal rights and opportunities

genderfluid – describes someone who does not have a fixed identity as male or female

heterosexual – being sexually attracted to people of the opposite sex

hierarchy – a system where people are ranked according to their status

homosexuality – when people are sexually attracted to people of the same sex

hypermasculinity – exaggerated male behaviour, including an emphasis on strength

intersex – people whose bodies do not fit the usual definitions for male or female

liberalism – a way of thinking about the world that is willing to accept behaviour or opinions that are different from your own

machismo – machismo and macho are Spanish and Portugeuse words now used in English to describe agressive masculinity

masculinity politics – how masculinity fits into society

patriarchy, patriarchal – a social system in which men are in control

pejorative – a way of describing something that conveys disapproval or a lack of respect for it

republican – describes someone who is the opposite of a monarchist. In the Irish context, it is someone who wishes all of Ireland were free from British rule and free from any association with the British monarchy.

segregated schooling – in 1940s USA, this meant black and white children being educated in separate schools. In Belfast, this means Catholic and Protestant children attending separate schools.

socialisation – the process of learning to behave in a way that society thinks is acceptable

Soviet Union – the Union of Soviet Socialist Republics, formed of Russia and 14 other republics, which lasted from 1922 to 1991

status – the position of something or someone compared to something or someone else

stereotype – a fixed, simplified idea about a person or thing that is not necessarily true, but is widely believed to be true

taboo – something that is not talked about because it is thought to be very wrong or controversial

trans – describes people who do not feel they are the same gender as the body they were born with

FURTHER INFORMATION

The Campaign Against Living Miserably (CALM) is an award-winning charity dedicated to preventing male suicide.

Helpline number: 0800 58 58 58
www.thecalmzone.net

Childline offers a free, private and confidental service to anyone in the UK under the age of 19 who is worried or needs help.

Childline helpline number: 0800 1111
www.childline.org.uk

Read about how Time to Change is working to change the way we all think and act about mental health problems:
www.time-to-change.org.uk/about-us

For inclusive (and non-sexist!) books, visit Letterbox Library:
www.letterboxlibrary.com

Read about the Let Toys Be Toys and the Let Books Be Books campaigns at:
http://lettoysbetoys.org.uk

WHAT **DO YOU** THINK?

Hopefully, this book has helped you to think about what masculinity is and how it affects us all. The following talking points will help you go further with your own ideas:

Does masculinity make it hard to be a man, woman, boy or girl?

Who benefits most from masculinity?

Who benefits least from masculinity?

Where can you see the effects of masculinity?

Does masculinity affect how we think?

What are the best things about masculinity?

What are the worst things about masculinity?

INDEX